Writers Edge
2025 EDITION

MASTERING THE ART OF THE SALES PITCH

Multi-Award-Winning-Author
B Alan Bourgeois

Art of the Sales Pitch

B Alan Bourgeois

Mastering the Art of the Sales Pitch

© B Alan Bourgeois 2025

All rights reserved. No part of this publication may be reproduced, stored in a retrieval system, or transmitted in any form or by any means, electronic, mechanical, photocopying, recording, or otherwise, without the prior written permission of the publisher.

The information and opinions expressed in this book are believed to be accurate and reliable, but no responsibility or liability is assumed by the publisher for any errors, omissions, or any damages caused by the use of these products, procedures, or methods presented herein.

The book is sold and distributed on an "as is" basis without warranties of any kind, either expressed or implied, including but not limited to warranties of merchantability or fitness for a particular purpose. The purchaser or reader of this book assumes complete responsibility for the use of these materials and information.

Any legal disputes arising from the use of this book shall be governed by the laws of the jurisdiction where the book was purchased, without regard to its conflict of law provisions, and shall be resolved exclusively in the courts of that jurisdiction.

ISBN: 979-8-3483-9877-4

Publisher: Bourgeois Media & Consulting
(BourgeoisMedia.com)

Art of the Sales Pitch

B ALAN BOUERGEOIS

STORYTELLING
LITERACY & HERITAGE

Thank you for purchasing this limited edition book, offered in celebration of the author's 50-year milestone. Proceeds from your purchase support the Texas Authors Institute of History, a museum founded by the author in 2015, dedicated to preserving the legacy of Texas authors.

https://TexasAuthors.Institute

B Alan Bourgeois

Dear Fellow Authors,

I'm delighted to introduce this book—and every guide in this series—as a short, easy-to-read resource designed to help you succeed in your writing journey. As writers, our true passion lies in creating stories, and I understand that delving into the business side of publishing might not be where we wish to spend most of our time.

That's why I've made a conscious effort to keep things simple and straightforward, focusing on practical advice without unnecessary fluff. You'll find that some concepts overlap between books, and that's intentional—to reinforce key ideas and ensure that whichever guide you pick up, you're equipped with valuable tools to enhance your success.

I genuinely hope you find these guides enjoyable and helpful. Your feedback means the world to me, and I look forward to hearing about your experiences and triumphs.

Happy writing, and here's to your continued success!

Art of the Sales Pitch

Introduction

In today's competitive literary landscape, writing a compelling book is just the first step in an author's journey to success. The real challenge lies in effectively promoting your book and capturing the attention of readers, agents, and publishers. Crafting a persuasive and engaging sales pitch is essential for any author seeking to stand out in the crowded marketplace. "**Mastering the Art of the Sales Pitch**" is your comprehensive guide to navigating this critical aspect of the writing profession. Whether you're a debut author or a seasoned writer, this book offers practical strategies, proven techniques, and insightful tips to help you create and deliver powerful sales pitches that resonate with your target audience.

Why Focus on the Sales Pitch?
A well-crafted sales pitch can make all the difference between your book being overlooked or becoming a bestseller. It's not just about selling your book; it's about conveying your passion, highlighting your unique value, and connecting with your audience on an emotional level. A great pitch can open doors to new opportunities, from securing a literary agent to landing a publishing deal and ultimately reaching more readers.

What You Will Learn
This book is structured around ten essential strategies that will equip you with the skills and knowledge needed to master the art of the sales pitch. Each chapter delves into a specific aspect of pitching, offering detailed guidance, real-world examples, and actionable advice. Here's a glimpse of what you can expect:
1. **Identify Your Target Audience:** Learn how to pinpoint who your readers are and tailor your pitch to their interests and needs.

2. **Highlight the Unique Value of Your Book:** Discover how to emphasize what sets your book apart and why readers should choose it over others.
3. **Use Emotional Language:** Harness the power of emotions to create a deep connection with your audience.
4. **Be Concise and to the Point:** Master the art of delivering a clear, focused, and impactful pitch.
5. **Practice Your Pitch:** Develop the confidence and finesse needed to deliver your pitch smoothly and persuasively.
6. **Use Social Proof:** Leverage reviews, testimonials, and endorsements to build credibility and trust.
7. **Include a Call-to-Action:** Learn how to motivate your audience to take the next step, whether it's buying your book or visiting your website.
8. **Use Visuals:** Enhance your pitch with compelling visuals that capture attention and convey your message.
9. **Tailor Your Pitch to the Audience:** Adapt your pitch to resonate with different audiences and contexts.
10. **Be Authentic:** Embrace your unique voice and personal story to create a genuine and relatable pitch.

Additional Insights

Beyond these ten core strategies, you'll also find bonus chapters and tips on related topics, such as understanding market trends, developing a strong opening, addressing potential objections, leveraging networking opportunities, utilizing digital platforms, and continuously measuring and improving your efforts.

Who This Book Is For

"Mastering the Art of the Sales Pitch" is designed for authors at all stages of their writing careers. Whether you're preparing to pitch your first book or looking to refine your existing approach, this book provides valuable insights and practical tools to help you succeed. Literary agents, publishers, and marketers will

Art of the Sales Pitch

also find it a useful resource for understanding what makes a compelling pitch.

Your Journey to Mastery
Crafting an effective sales pitch is both an art and a science. It requires creativity, empathy, and a strategic approach. This book aims to demystify the process and empower you with the knowledge and confidence to present your book in the best possible light.

As you embark on this journey, remember that your pitch is an extension of your passion for your book. By applying the strategies and techniques outlined in this book, you'll be well on your way to mastering the art of the sales pitch and achieving greater success as an author.

Let's begin this journey together, and unlock the full potential of your book with a pitch that captivates, convinces, and compels.

Chapters

1. Identify Your Target Audience — 10
2. Highlight the Unique Value of Your Book — 15
3. Use Emotional Language — 19
4. Be Concise and to the Point. — 23
5. Practice Your Pitch — 27
6. Use Social Proof — 31
7. Include a Call-to-Action — 35
8. Use Visuals — 39
9. Tailor Your Pitch to the Audience — 43
10. Be Authentic — 47
11. What is an Elevator Pitch? — 51
12. Understand the Market — 55
13. Develop a Strong Opening — 59
14. Address Potential Objections — 63
15. Leverage Networking Opportunities — 67
16. Utilize Digital Platforms — 71
17. Measure and Improve — 75

About the Author — 79
Other Books from the Author in this Series — 80

1
Identify Your Target Audience

When it comes to promoting a book, identifying your target audience is crucial. Understanding who your readers are and what motivates them can help you create a sales pitch that speaks directly to their needs and interests. Here are some key considerations for identifying your target audience and tailoring your sales pitch accordingly:

Define Your Genre:
Start by identifying the genre of your book. This will help you understand the type of reader who is most likely to be interested in your work. Genres can range from romance, science fiction, and fantasy to self-help, biographies, and historical non-fiction. Each genre has its unique audience with specific expectations and preferences. For instance, readers of romance novels might look for emotional connection and happy endings, while science fiction enthusiasts might be drawn to futuristic concepts and technological innovations.

> **Example:** If you have written a historical fiction novel, your target audience might include history buffs, readers interested in specific historical periods, and fans of intricate, well-researched storytelling.

Research Your Competition:
Look at the other authors in your genre who are successful and identify their target audience. This can give you a good starting point for understanding your readership. Analyze their marketing strategies, the tone of their pitches, and the feedback they receive from readers. Competitor analysis can provide insights into what works and what doesn't in your genre.

Example: Study how bestselling authors in your genre market their books. What kind of language do they use? What elements do they emphasize in their pitches? This information can guide you in crafting your own pitch.

Consider Your Book's Themes and Subject Matter:
Think about the themes and subject matter of your book. Who would be most interested in these topics? Are there any groups or communities that would be particularly interested in what you have to say? Themes such as love, adventure, overcoming adversity, or self-improvement can attract different kinds of readers.

Example: If your book addresses mental health issues, your target audience might include individuals interested in psychology, self-help enthusiasts, and those personally affected by mental health challenges.

Think About Demographics:
Consider factors such as age, gender, occupation, and location. Depending on the subject matter of your book, certain demographics may be more likely to be interested in your work. Demographics can greatly influence how you shape your pitch and where you choose to promote your book.

Example: A young adult fantasy novel might appeal to teenagers and young adults, primarily aged 12-18. Understanding this can help you focus your marketing efforts on platforms and communities where this age group is most active, such as social media sites like Instagram and TikTok.

Look at Reader Reviews:
Look at reviews of your book on websites such as Amazon or Goodreads to see who is reading and enjoying your work.

Art of the Sales Pitch

This can give you valuable insights into your target audience. Pay attention to common themes in the reviews, such as the aspects of your book that readers praise the most.

Example: If multiple reviews highlight the strong female protagonist in your novel, you might consider targeting readers who are looking for empowering female characters in their reading material.

Tailoring Your Sales Pitch:
Once you have a good understanding of your target audience, you can begin to tailor your sales pitch to their interests and needs. Here are some key tips for doing so:

1. **Use Language That Resonates with Your Audience:** Use the language and terminology that your target audience is familiar with. This will help you connect with them more effectively. If your audience is tech-savvy, incorporate relevant jargon and concepts.

    Example: For a sci-fi audience, use terms like "cybernetics," "quantum mechanics," and "space exploration" to pique their interest.

2. **Highlight the Benefits of Your Book:** Emphasize the specific benefits that your book offers to your target audience. What problems does it solve? What questions does it answer? Make sure to align these benefits with your audience's needs and desires.

    Example: For a self-help book on time management, highlight how it can help readers organize their lives, reduce stress, and increase productivity.

3. **Speak to Their Emotions:** Use emotional language that connects with your target audience. People are more likely to buy a book that makes them feel something. Whether it's

excitement, curiosity, empathy, or hope, emotions can drive purchasing decisions.

> **Example:** If your book is a romance novel, evoke emotions of love, passion, and heartache in your pitch to draw readers in.

4. **Use Examples and Anecdotes That Resonate with Your Audience:** Use examples and anecdotes that are relevant to your target audience's experiences. This will help them connect with your book on a deeper level. Real-life stories or relatable scenarios can make your pitch more engaging and memorable.

   > **Example:** For a book on entrepreneurship, share success stories of entrepreneurs who started from scratch and built successful businesses, mirroring the journey your readers aspire to undertake.

5. **Make It Clear Why Your Book Is Unique:** Emphasize what sets your book apart from others in your genre. What makes it different? What makes it special? Your unique selling proposition (USP) should be front and center in your pitch.

   > **Example:** If your mystery novel features an innovative plot structure or a groundbreaking twist, highlight this uniqueness to intrigue potential readers.

By identifying your target audience and tailoring your sales pitch to their interests and needs, you can create a compelling message that resonates with readers and drives sales. Remember, the key to a successful sales pitch is understanding your audience and speaking directly to their motivations and desires.

Chapter Summary: In this chapter, we explored the importance of identifying your target audience and tailoring your sales pitch

Art of the Sales Pitch

to resonate with them. By defining your genre, researching your competition, considering your book's themes and subject matter, thinking about demographics, and looking at reader reviews, you can gain valuable insights into your audience. With these insights, you can craft a pitch that uses language, highlights benefits, speaks to emotions, includes relevant examples, and emphasizes the uniqueness of your book, ultimately driving engagement and sales.

2
Highlight the Unique Value of Your Book

When crafting a sales pitch, it is essential to emphasize what sets your book apart from others in its genre. Highlighting the unique value of your book can capture the interest of potential readers and convince them to choose your work over others. Here's how to identify and showcase the distinctive qualities of your book effectively:

Identify Your Unique Selling Proposition (USP):
Your USP is the unique benefit or feature that distinguishes your book from the competition. It could be an innovative plot twist, an unconventional narrative style, exclusive insights, or a fresh perspective on a common theme. Determine what makes your book special and how it provides value to readers.

> **Example:** If your book is a mystery novel with an interactive component where readers can solve puzzles along with the protagonist, this interactive feature could be your USP.

Understand Your Book's Core Message:
Every book has a core message or theme that it conveys. Understanding this message can help you articulate the unique value of your book. Think about the primary takeaway or the central idea your book aims to communicate.

> **Example:** A self-help book might have a core message about the importance of resilience and overcoming obstacles. Highlighting this theme can attract readers who are seeking inspiration and practical advice on personal growth.

Art of the Sales Pitch

Showcase Your Expertise:
If your book draws on your personal expertise or experience, make sure to highlight this in your pitch. Readers often look for authors who are credible and knowledgeable in their field. Your background can add significant value to your book.

> **Example:** If you are a seasoned psychologist writing a book on mental health, your professional experience and insights can be a major selling point. Emphasize how your expertise provides readers with reliable and valuable information.

Highlight Unique Content and Features:
Identify any unique content or features in your book that set it apart. This could include original research, exclusive interviews, unique characters, or innovative storytelling techniques. Anything that adds value and differentiates your book should be highlighted in your pitch.

> **Example:** If your historical novel includes meticulously researched details about a little-known event, emphasize this aspect to attract history enthusiasts who value accuracy and depth.

Use Comparative Positioning:
Position your book in relation to other successful books in your genre. Highlight what makes your book similar to these popular titles but also emphasize how it differs. This can help potential readers see why they might enjoy your book while also appreciating its unique qualities.

> **Example:** "If you loved 'Gone Girl,' you'll be captivated by the psychological twists and dark secrets in my thriller, but with a unique narrative that dives deeper into the protagonist's psyche."

Use Testimonials and Endorsements:
Incorporate testimonials and endorsements from readers, experts, or influencers who can vouch for the unique value of your book. Positive feedback from credible sources can add significant weight to your pitch.

> **Example:** Include a quote from a well-known author or a respected critic praising the originality and impact of your book. This can help build trust and credibility with potential readers.

Emphasize Reader Benefits:
Clearly articulate the benefits readers will gain from your book. What problems does it solve? What knowledge or entertainment value does it provide? Make sure these benefits are tied to the unique aspects of your book.

> **Example:** For a cookbook with a focus on quick and healthy meals, emphasize how it helps busy individuals prepare nutritious dishes in a short amount of time, offering convenience and health benefits.

Crafting Your Pitch:
With these elements in mind, craft a pitch that succinctly highlights the unique value of your book. Ensure your pitch is clear, compelling, and focuses on the aspects that set your book apart.

> **Example Pitch:** "Unlock the secrets of time management with 'Efficient Living,' a revolutionary guide by renowned productivity expert Jane Doe. Unlike other self-help books, 'Efficient Living' combines cutting-edge research with practical exercises that can be completed in just 10 minutes a day. Packed with exclusive tips from top CEOs and real-life success stories, this book is your ultimate tool for achieving more with less stress."

Art of the Sales Pitch

Chapter Summary: In this chapter, we discussed the importance of highlighting the unique value of your book in your sales pitch. By identifying your unique selling proposition, understanding your book's core message, showcasing your expertise, highlighting unique content and features, using comparative positioning, incorporating testimonials and endorsements, and emphasizing reader benefits, you can create a compelling and differentiated pitch that attracts potential readers. Your pitch should clearly communicate what makes your book special and why readers should choose it over others in its genre.

3
Use Emotional Language

Emotion is a powerful motivator in the decision-making process. When crafting a sales pitch for your book, using emotional language can help create a strong connection with your audience, making them more likely to be interested in and purchase your book. Here's how to effectively incorporate emotional language into your sales pitch:

Understand the Emotions You Want to Evoke:
Different genres and themes evoke different emotions. Understand the primary emotions your book is designed to elicit and use them to shape your pitch. Common emotions include excitement, curiosity, fear, joy, empathy, and inspiration.

> **Example:** A thriller might evoke excitement and fear, while a romance novel might focus on love and joy.

Use Vivid Descriptions:
Descriptive language can help paint a vivid picture in the reader's mind, making the emotional appeal stronger. Use sensory details and powerful adjectives to bring your pitch to life.

> **Example:** "Dive into a world of suspense with 'The Silent Witness,' where every page is drenched in tension and every twist leaves you breathless. Feel the protagonist's heart race as danger lurks around every corner."

Share Personal Anecdotes:
Personal stories and anecdotes can create an emotional connection with your audience. Sharing a meaningful story

Art of the Sales Pitch

related to your book can make your pitch more relatable and engaging.

> **Example:** "Inspired by my own journey of overcoming adversity, 'Rising from the Ashes' is a testament to the power of resilience and hope. Through the protagonist's struggles and triumphs, readers will find a piece of their own story."

Tap into Universal Themes:
Universal themes such as love, loss, adventure, and redemption resonate with a wide audience. Highlight these themes in your pitch to connect with readers on an emotional level.

> **Example:** "At its heart, 'The Lost Melody' is a story of love and loss, a journey through grief that ultimately leads to healing and rediscovery."

Use Relatable Characters:
Characters that readers can relate to emotionally can make your pitch more compelling. Highlight the emotional journeys of your characters and how readers might see themselves in these stories.

> **Example:** "Follow Emma's journey in 'Uncharted Waters,' as she navigates the turbulent seas of self-discovery and love. Her struggles and triumphs will resonate with anyone who has ever felt lost or out of place."

Create a Sense of Urgency:
Using emotional language to create a sense of urgency can prompt readers to take immediate action. Words that convey scarcity, time-sensitivity, or high stakes can heighten emotional engagement.

> **Example:** "Don't miss out on the book that everyone is talking about. 'Eclipse of the Heart' is a limited edition release, and it's flying off the shelves. Get your copy before it's too late!"

Use Powerful Quotes and Testimonials:
Incorporate quotes and testimonials that evoke strong emotions. Positive feedback from readers who have been emotionally impacted by your book can be very persuasive.

> **Example:** "One reader said, 'I couldn't put it down. 'Beneath the Surface' had me laughing, crying, and gasping for breath. It's a rollercoaster of emotions that you won't soon forget.'"

Show Passion and Enthusiasm:
Your own passion and enthusiasm for your book can be infectious. Use emotive language to convey how much you care about your book and its message.

> **Example:** "Writing 'Whispers of the Past' was a labor of love. Every word, every scene was crafted with care and emotion. I can't wait for you to experience the magic and mystery that I poured my heart into."

Use Visual Language:
Visual language can help create emotional imagery in the reader's mind. Descriptions that invoke visual scenes or scenarios can make your pitch more engaging and memorable.

> **Example:** "Imagine standing on the edge of a cliff, the wind whipping around you, the vast ocean stretching out before you. That's the feeling you'll get when you dive into 'Edge of the Abyss,' a novel that takes you to the brink of adventure."

Art of the Sales Pitch

Combine Emotions for Greater Impact:
Combining multiple emotions can make your pitch more dynamic and impactful. Create a layered emotional experience by blending different feelings such as fear and hope, or sorrow and joy.

> **Example:** "Experience the heart-pounding suspense and the bittersweet beauty of 'The Last Echo.' This novel will take you on an emotional rollercoaster, leaving you breathless and inspired."

Chapter Summary: In this chapter, we explored the importance of using emotional language in your sales pitch. By understanding the emotions you want to evoke, using vivid descriptions, sharing personal anecdotes, tapping into universal themes, highlighting relatable characters, creating a sense of urgency, incorporating powerful quotes and testimonials, showing passion and enthusiasm, using visual language, and combining emotions for greater impact, you can create a compelling and emotionally resonant pitch. Emotionally engaging your audience can make them more likely to connect with your book and take action.

4
Be Concise and to the Point

A sales pitch should be short, focused, and easy to understand. Avoid rambling or going off on tangents. Conciseness and clarity are key to making a strong impression and holding your audience's attention. Here's how to craft a concise and impactful sales pitch:

Focus on the Essentials:
Identify the most important points you need to convey about your book. These should include the genre, the main plot or theme, the unique selling proposition, and the benefits for the reader. Eliminate any unnecessary details that don't directly support these points.

> **Example:** "Discover the untold story of 'The Forgotten Kingdom,' a historical fiction novel that takes you deep into the mysteries of ancient civilizations. Perfect for history enthusiasts and adventure seekers alike."

Use Clear and Simple Language:
Avoid using complex or technical language that might confuse your audience. Aim for clarity and simplicity in your pitch. Your goal is to communicate your message as effectively as possible.

> **Example:** Instead of saying, "This book delineates the intricate socio-political dynamics of a bygone era," say, "This book explores the complex relationships and power struggles of ancient societies."

Art of the Sales Pitch

Structure Your Pitch:
Organize your pitch in a logical order. Start with a hook to grab attention, followed by a brief overview of your book, its unique aspects, and a clear call-to-action. A well-structured pitch is easier to follow and more engaging.

Example Structure:
1. **Hook:** "Are you ready for an adventure that will transport you back in time?"
2. **Overview:** "'The Forgotten Kingdom' is a captivating historical fiction novel set in ancient Mesopotamia."
3. **Unique Aspects:** "With rich, meticulously researched details and a plot full of twists and turns, this book offers a unique glimpse into a lost world."
4. **Call-to-Action:** "Get your copy today and embark on a journey through history."

Avoid Redundancy:
Ensure that each word and sentence in your pitch adds value. Avoid repeating the same points or using filler words. Every sentence should contribute to building interest and excitement about your book.

Example: Instead of saying, "This book is great and wonderful and has many exciting parts," say, "This book offers a thrilling adventure with every chapter packed with excitement."

Use Bullet Points:
When appropriate, use bullet points to list key features or benefits. Bullet points are easy to read and help to break down information into digestible chunks.

Example:
- Engaging plot with unexpected twists

- Rich historical details based on extensive research
- Complex, relatable characters
- A journey through ancient civilizations

Practice Precision:
Practice delivering your pitch until you can do it smoothly and confidently within a short timeframe, ideally under a minute. Precision comes with practice and refining your message to its core components.

> **Example:** Record yourself delivering your pitch and aim to keep it within a 60-second limit. Listen back to identify any areas where you can be more concise or impactful.

Tailor Your Pitch:
Adapt your pitch to the specific audience and context. Tailoring your message to suit different platforms, such as social media, email marketing, or face-to-face interactions, can enhance its effectiveness.

> **Example:** For a social media post, keep it brief and visually engaging: "Unlock the secrets of 'The Forgotten Kingdom.' Dive into a world of mystery and adventure. Available now!"

Use Strong, Active Verbs:
Active verbs make your pitch more dynamic and engaging. Avoid passive constructions and aim for direct, compelling language.

> **Example:** Instead of saying, "The story is told through the eyes of a young archaeologist," say, "Join a young archaeologist as she unearths the secrets of 'The Forgotten Kingdom.'"

Provide a Clear Call-to-Action:
End your pitch with a clear and compelling call-to-action. Tell your audience exactly what you want them to do next,

Art of the Sales Pitch

whether it's buying your book, visiting your website, or signing up for your newsletter.

> **Example:** "Don't miss out on this unforgettable adventure. Buy 'The Forgotten Kingdom' today and step back in time!"

Edit and Refine:
Review your pitch multiple times and refine it for clarity, brevity, and impact. Get feedback from others and make adjustments as needed to ensure your message is as strong as possible.

> **Example:** Share your pitch with friends, colleagues, or fellow authors and ask for their input. Use their feedback to polish and perfect your pitch.

Chapter Summary: In this chapter, we discussed the importance of being concise and to the point in your sales pitch. By focusing on the essentials, using clear and simple language, structuring your pitch effectively, avoiding redundancy, using bullet points, practicing precision, tailoring your pitch, using strong active verbs, providing a clear call-to-action, and editing and refining your message, you can create a concise and impactful pitch. A well-crafted, concise pitch can capture your audience's attention and make a strong impression, driving interest and sales for your book.

5
Practice Your Pitch

Delivering a smooth, confident, and engaging pitch requires practice. The more you practice, the more natural and persuasive your pitch will become. Here's how to effectively practice and refine your sales pitch:

Start with a Script:
Begin by writing a script for your pitch. Include all the key points you want to cover, and structure it in a logical and engaging way. Your script should serve as a foundation that you can refine and adjust as needed.

> **Example:** "Are you ready for an adventure? 'The Forgotten Kingdom' takes you on a journey through ancient Mesopotamia, uncovering secrets and solving mysteries. With rich historical details and a captivating plot, this book is a must-read for history enthusiasts and adventure lovers alike. Get your copy today and step back in time!"

Practice Aloud:
Practice delivering your pitch out loud. This helps you get comfortable with the words and identify any awkward or unclear phrases. Speaking aloud can also help you gauge the timing of your pitch.

> **Example:** Stand in front of a mirror and deliver your pitch, paying attention to your tone, pace, and body language.

Art of the Sales Pitch

Record Yourself:
Recording yourself can provide valuable feedback on your delivery. Listen to the recording to identify areas for improvement, such as pacing, tone, and emphasis. Make adjustments based on what you hear.

> **Example:** Use your smartphone or a recording device to capture your pitch. Listen for any hesitations or areas where you can be more dynamic and engaging.

Get Feedback:
Share your pitch with friends, family, or colleagues and ask for their honest feedback. They can provide insights into how clear and compelling your pitch is, and suggest areas for improvement.

> **Example:** Ask a friend to listen to your pitch and provide constructive criticism. They might suggest emphasizing certain points more or adjusting your tone for better engagement.

Refine Your Script:
Based on the feedback you receive and your own observations, refine your script. Make sure it flows smoothly and effectively communicates the key points. Aim for a balance between conciseness and detail.

> **Example:** If your feedback indicates that the beginning of your pitch is too slow, adjust your script to start with a more dynamic hook.

Memorize Key Points:
While you don't need to memorize your pitch word-for-word, it's important to have the key points firmly in your mind. This allows you to deliver your pitch naturally and confidently, without relying too heavily on your script.

> **Example:** Focus on memorizing the main sections of your pitch: the hook, the overview, the unique aspects, and the call-to-action. This way, you can speak more freely and adapt as needed.

Practice in Different Contexts:
Practice delivering your pitch in various settings, such as in front of a mirror, to a small group, or in a more formal presentation. This helps you become comfortable pitching in different environments and to different audiences.

> **Example:** Practice your pitch during a writers' group meeting or at a local book club. This will help you gain confidence and adjust your delivery based on audience reactions.

Focus on Your Delivery:
Pay attention to your tone, pace, and body language. Speak clearly and at a moderate pace, making sure to emphasize key points. Use gestures and facial expressions to enhance your message and engage your audience.

> **Example:** Use a confident, enthusiastic tone to convey your passion for your book. Make eye contact with your audience and use natural gestures to emphasize important points.

Be Prepared for Questions:
Anticipate questions your audience might have and prepare responses. Being able to answer questions confidently can enhance your credibility and make your pitch more persuasive.

> **Example:** If someone asks about the historical accuracy of your book, be ready to explain your research process and the sources you used to ensure authenticity.

Art of the Sales Pitch

Practice Regularly:
Regular practice is key to mastering your pitch. The more you practice, the more confident and polished you will become. Set aside time each week to practice and refine your pitch.

> **Example:** Dedicate 15-20 minutes each day to practice your pitch. Over time, you'll notice improvements in your delivery and confidence.

Chapter Summary: In this chapter, we discussed the importance of practicing your pitch to deliver it smoothly and confidently. By starting with a script, practicing aloud, recording yourself, getting feedback, refining your script, memorizing key points, practicing in different contexts, focusing on your delivery, being prepared for questions, and practicing regularly, you can create a compelling and polished pitch. Regular practice helps you become more natural and persuasive, increasing the chances of engaging your audience and driving sales for your book.

6
Use Social Proof

Social proof is a powerful tool in building credibility and persuading potential readers to choose your book. By showcasing reviews, testimonials, and endorsements from satisfied readers or industry experts, you can demonstrate the value and appeal of your book. Here's how to effectively use social proof in your sales pitch:

Gather Reviews and Testimonials:
Actively seek out reviews and testimonials from readers, bloggers, critics, and influencers. These can be collected from platforms like Amazon, Goodreads, and social media. Positive feedback from others can significantly enhance your pitch.

> **Example:** After your book launch, encourage readers to leave reviews on Amazon and Goodreads. Reach out to book bloggers and ask if they'd be willing to review your book.

Highlight Positive Feedback:
Incorporate the best and most impactful reviews and testimonials into your pitch. Highlight quotes that emphasize the unique strengths and benefits of your book. Make sure to include the name and, if possible, the credentials of the person providing the testimonial.

> **Example:** "A riveting page-turner! 'The Forgotten Kingdom' is a masterpiece of historical fiction." – John Smith, New York Times bestselling author.

Art of the Sales Pitch

Use Endorsements from Experts:
Endorsements from respected figures in your genre or industry can add significant credibility to your book. Reach out to authors, academics, or professionals who might be willing to endorse your work.

> **Example:** "An extraordinary journey through time. A must-read for history enthusiasts." – Dr. Jane Doe, Professor of History at XYZ University.

Showcase Awards and Recognitions:
If your book has received any awards, recognitions, or notable mentions, be sure to include these in your pitch. Awards and recognitions can serve as strong indicators of quality and value.

> **Example:** "Winner of the 2024 Historical Fiction Award. 'The Forgotten Kingdom' has been recognized for its exceptional storytelling and historical accuracy."

Incorporate Star Ratings:
Star ratings provide a quick and visual indication of your book's popularity and quality. Highlight the average star rating from platforms like Amazon or Goodreads in your pitch.

> **Example:** "Rated 4.8 stars on Amazon. 'The Forgotten Kingdom' is beloved by readers for its gripping narrative and rich historical detail."

Use Visuals to Enhance Social Proof:
Visuals can make social proof more engaging and memorable. Use graphics, images, and videos to showcase reviews, testimonials, and endorsements. Consider creating infographics or video testimonials to add visual appeal.

Example: Create a graphic that features a five-star rating along with a quote from a positive review. Share this on social media and include it in your promotional materials.

Share Reader Stories:
Sharing stories from readers who have been positively impacted by your book can create an emotional connection and build trust. Highlight how your book has helped or inspired readers.

Example: "After reading 'The Forgotten Kingdom,' I felt a renewed sense of curiosity about ancient history. This book sparked a passion in me that I never knew I had." – Sarah, avid reader.

Leverage Social Media:
Use social media platforms to share reviews, testimonials, and endorsements. Encourage readers to post about your book and tag you. Reposting and engaging with these posts can amplify your social proof.

Example: Share screenshots of positive reviews on Instagram and Twitter. Use hashtags and tag the reviewers to increase visibility and engagement.

Feature Social Proof Prominently:
Make sure social proof is prominently featured in your sales pitch and marketing materials. Place reviews, testimonials, and endorsements in visible locations on your website, book cover, and promotional content.

Example: Include a section on your website dedicated to reader testimonials and expert endorsements. Feature quotes on the back cover of your book and in the blurb.

Art of the Sales Pitch

Update Social Proof Regularly:
As you receive new reviews and endorsements, update your pitch and marketing materials to reflect the latest and most relevant feedback. Regularly refreshing your social proof can keep your pitch current and credible.

Example: Periodically check for new reviews on Amazon and Goodreads. Update your website and promotional materials with the latest positive feedback.

Chapter Summary: In this chapter, we explored the importance of using social proof to build credibility and persuade potential readers. By gathering reviews and testimonials, highlighting positive feedback, using endorsements from experts, showcasing awards and recognitions, incorporating star ratings, using visuals to enhance social proof, sharing reader stories, leveraging social media, featuring social proof prominently, and updating it regularly, you can effectively use social proof in your sales pitch. Social proof can significantly enhance the perceived value of your book and increase the likelihood of engaging and convincing potential readers.

7
Include a Call-to-Action

A clear and compelling call-to-action (CTA) is a crucial component of any effective sales pitch. It directs your audience on what to do next, encouraging them to take the desired action. Here's how to craft and incorporate a powerful CTA into your pitch:

Be Clear and Direct:
Your CTA should be clear and unambiguous. Tell your audience exactly what you want them to do, whether it's buying your book, visiting your website, signing up for a newsletter, or following you on social media.

> **Example:** "Buy your copy of 'The Forgotten Kingdom' today and embark on an unforgettable journey through ancient history."

Use Action-Oriented Language:
Use strong, action-oriented verbs to motivate your audience. Words like "buy," "download," "subscribe," "join," and "discover" can create a sense of urgency and prompt immediate action.

> **Example:** "Download the first chapter for free and discover the mysteries of 'The Forgotten Kingdom'."

Highlight the Benefits:
Emphasize the benefits of taking the desired action. Explain what the audience will gain or experience by following your CTA. This helps reinforce the value and encourages them to act.

Art of the Sales Pitch

> **Example:** "Join our newsletter and get exclusive access to behind-the-scenes content, author insights, and special discounts."

Create a Sense of Urgency:
Incorporate elements that create a sense of urgency or scarcity. Limited-time offers, exclusive content, and early bird discounts can prompt your audience to act quickly.

> **Example:** "Hurry! Get 20% off your purchase of 'The Forgotten Kingdom' for a limited time only."

Keep It Simple:
Avoid overwhelming your audience with multiple CTAs. Focus on one clear and straightforward action you want them to take. This helps prevent confusion and increases the likelihood of them following through.

> **Example:** "Click the link below to buy your copy now."

Position Your CTA Strategically:
Place your CTA in a prominent position where it's easily noticeable. It should be at the end of your pitch or in a location where it naturally follows the flow of your message.

> **Example:** "After learning about the thrilling adventure in 'The Forgotten Kingdom,' click here to purchase your copy and start reading today."

Test Different CTAs:
Experiment with different CTAs to see which ones resonate best with your audience. A/B testing can help you determine the most effective phrasing, placement, and format for your CTAs.

Example: Test variations like "Get Your Copy Now," "Order Today," and "Start Reading Now" to see which generates the most clicks and conversions.

Use Multiple Channels:
Incorporate your CTA across various marketing channels, such as your website, social media, email newsletters, and promotional materials. Consistent messaging across platforms can reinforce your CTA and increase its effectiveness.

Example: Include a CTA in your email signature, social media bios, and on your book's landing page.

Personalize Your CTA:
Personalize your CTA to make it more relevant and appealing to your audience. Tailoring your message to specific segments or individual preferences can enhance engagement.

Example: "Hey [Name], ready for an adventure? Click here to start reading 'The Forgotten Kingdom' and uncover its secrets."

Follow Up:
After your audience takes the desired action, follow up with additional engagement. Thank them for their support, provide further value, and encourage continued interaction with your content and brand.

Example: After someone subscribes to your newsletter, send a personalized welcome email thanking them and offering a free chapter or exclusive content as a token of appreciation.

Chapter Summary: In this chapter, we discussed the importance of including a clear and compelling call-to-action

Art of the Sales Pitch

(CTA) in your sales pitch. By being clear and direct, using action-oriented language, highlighting the benefits, creating a sense of urgency, keeping it simple, positioning your CTA strategically, testing different CTAs, using multiple channels, personalizing your CTA, and following up with your audience, you can craft effective CTAs that encourage your audience to take the desired action. A well-crafted CTA can drive engagement and conversions, helping you achieve your marketing goals.

8
Use Visuals

Visuals are a powerful tool in capturing attention and enhancing the impact of your sales pitch. By incorporating images, graphics, and other visual elements, you can make your pitch more engaging and memorable. Here's how to effectively use visuals in your sales pitch:

Choose High-Quality Images:
Use high-quality images that are visually appealing and relevant to your book. These can include the book cover, illustrations, and images that represent themes or scenes from your book.

> **Example:** Include a high-resolution image of your book cover in your pitch materials. This helps create a professional and polished presentation.

Create Visual Content:
Create visual content such as infographics, charts, and graphics that highlight key points or features of your book. Visual content can help break up text and make complex information more digestible.

> **Example:** Design an infographic that outlines the main plot points or characters in your book. This can serve as a quick reference for potential readers.

Use Video Trailers:
Consider creating a video trailer for your book. A well-produced trailer can capture the essence of your book and generate excitement. Share the trailer on your website, social media, and other promotional platforms.

Art of the Sales Pitch

> **Example:** Produce a short, 60-second trailer that introduces the main characters and setting of your book, accompanied by dramatic music and visuals.

Incorporate Quotes and Testimonials:
Use visuals to highlight quotes and testimonials from readers, critics, or influencers. Design graphics that feature these quotes prominently, making them stand out and enhancing their impact.

> **Example:** Create a graphic with a glowing review quote overlaid on an image related to your book's theme or setting.

Use Visual Consistency:
Ensure visual consistency across all your promotional materials. Use a cohesive color scheme, fonts, and design elements that align with your book's cover and branding. Consistent visuals help create a professional and recognizable brand image.

> **Example:** If your book cover features a specific color palette, use the same colors in your social media graphics and promotional content.

Create Shareable Content:
Design visuals that are easily shareable on social media platforms. Shareable content can increase your book's visibility and reach a wider audience. Include social media handles and hashtags to encourage sharing.

> **Example:** Create visually appealing quote graphics or snippets from your book that readers can share on Instagram, Twitter, or Facebook.

Use Visuals to Highlight Key Messages:
Use visuals to emphasize key messages or unique aspects of your book. Graphics can help draw attention to important points and make your pitch more persuasive.

> **Example:** If your book includes unique features like interactive elements or exclusive content, use visuals to highlight these features in your pitch.

Optimize for Different Platforms:
Ensure your visuals are optimized for different platforms and devices. Images and videos should be clear and properly formatted for mobile devices, desktops, and social media platforms.

> **Example:** Create multiple versions of your book cover image, resized and optimized for use on your website, Instagram, Facebook, and Twitter.

Engage with Visual Stories:
Use visuals to tell a story about your book. Storytelling through visuals can be a powerful way to connect with your audience and convey the essence of your book.

> **Example:** Create a series of images or a short video that tells a mini-story related to your book's plot or characters, leaving viewers curious and wanting more.

Measure Visual Impact:
Track the performance of your visual content to understand what resonates best with your audience. Use analytics tools to measure engagement, shares, and conversions, and adjust your visual strategy accordingly.

> **Example:** Monitor the engagement metrics on your social media posts featuring visuals. Identify which types

Art of the Sales Pitch

of images or videos receive the most likes, comments, and shares.

Chapter Summary: In this chapter, we explored the importance of using visuals to enhance your sales pitch. By choosing high-quality images, creating visual content, using video trailers, incorporating quotes and testimonials, ensuring visual consistency, creating shareable content, highlighting key messages with visuals, optimizing for different platforms, engaging with visual stories, and measuring visual impact, you can make your pitch more engaging and memorable. Visuals can capture attention and effectively convey the unique aspects and value of your book, increasing the likelihood of engaging potential readers and driving sales.

9
Tailor Your Pitch to the Audience

Adapting your sales pitch to the specific interests and needs of your audience can help you connect with them more effectively. By tailoring your message, you can make your pitch more relevant and engaging. Here's how to tailor your pitch to different audiences:

Understand Your Audience:
Conduct research to understand the demographics, preferences, and pain points of your audience. Use this information to customize your pitch. Consider factors such as age, gender, occupation, interests, and reading habits.

> **Example:** If your target audience is young adults, use language, themes, and references that resonate with their experiences and interests.

Segment Your Audience:
Divide your audience into segments based on specific characteristics or preferences. Tailor your pitch to each segment to address their unique needs and interests.

> **Example:** Create different pitches for various segments, such as young adult readers, history enthusiasts, and book club members. Each pitch should highlight aspects of your book that are most relevant to each segment.

Use Personalized Messaging:
Personalize your pitch to make it more relatable and impactful. Address your audience directly and use personalized language to create a connection.

Art of the Sales Pitch

> **Example:** Instead of a generic pitch, use a personalized approach: "Hey there, history buff! Ready for an adventure through ancient Mesopotamia? 'The Forgotten Kingdom' is just what you've been looking for."

Highlight Relevant Benefits:
Focus on the benefits that are most relevant to your audience. Explain how your book addresses their interests or solves their problems. Make sure these benefits are clearly communicated in your pitch.

> **Example:** For an audience interested in historical accuracy, emphasize the meticulous research and authentic details in your historical fiction novel.

Use Appropriate Channels:
Tailor your pitch to the platform or channel where you're delivering it. Different platforms require different approaches. Adjust your message and format to suit the medium.

> **Example:** On social media, use concise and visually appealing posts with hashtags and handles. In email newsletters, provide more detailed information and direct links to purchase.

Adjust Tone and Style:
Match the tone and style of your pitch to your audience's preferences. A formal tone may work for academic readers, while a casual and conversational tone may be better for a younger audience.

> **Example:** Use a professional tone when pitching to librarians or educators, and a more casual, engaging tone when addressing general readers or fans of the genre.

Incorporate Feedback:
Use feedback from your audience to refine and adjust your pitch. Listen to their responses and make changes based on what resonates most with them. Continuously improving your pitch can lead to better engagement.

>   **Example:** If you receive feedback that readers love the adventure elements of your book, emphasize these aspects more in future pitches.

Address Specific Interests:
Tailor your pitch to address the specific interests or hobbies of your audience. Connect your book to their passions to create a more compelling and relevant message.

>   **Example:** For an audience passionate about archaeology, highlight the archaeological discoveries and mysteries explored in your book.

Use Stories and Examples:
Incorporate stories and examples that resonate with your audience's experiences. Personal anecdotes or relatable scenarios can make your pitch more engaging and memorable.

>   **Example:** Share a story about how you were inspired to write your book by a historical event that your audience is likely to find intriguing.

Test and Iterate:
Experiment with different versions of your pitch and analyze the results. Testing different approaches can help you determine what works best for each audience segment. Use the insights gained to refine your pitch.

Art of the Sales Pitch

Example: Run A/B tests with different pitches on your website or social media ads. Track engagement metrics to see which version performs better.

Chapter Summary: In this chapter, we discussed the importance of tailoring your sales pitch to your audience. By understanding your audience, segmenting them, using personalized messaging, highlighting relevant benefits, using appropriate channels, adjusting tone and style, incorporating feedback, addressing specific interests, using stories and examples, and testing and iterating, you can create a pitch that resonates more effectively with different groups. Tailoring your pitch helps you connect with your audience on a deeper level, making your message more relevant and engaging, and increasing the chances of driving interest and sales for your book.

10
Be Authentic

Authenticity is key to creating a sincere and trustworthy sales pitch. Being genuine and true to yourself can help you build a connection with your audience and make your pitch more persuasive. Here's how to be authentic in your sales pitch:

Be Honest and Transparent:
Be honest about your book, its content, and its value. Avoid exaggerating or making unrealistic claims. Transparency builds trust and credibility with your audience.

> **Example:** If your book is a debut novel, embrace that fact and share your excitement about introducing your work to readers for the first time.

Share Your Passion:
Let your passion for your book and its message shine through. Authentic enthusiasm can be contagious and can inspire your audience to share in your excitement.

> **Example:** "Writing 'The Forgotten Kingdom' was a labor of love. I poured my heart into every page, and I can't wait for you to experience the adventure I've created."

Use Your Unique Voice:
Use your natural voice in your pitch. Avoid overly scripted or formal language that doesn't feel like you. Authenticity comes from being yourself and speaking in a way that feels natural to you.

Art of the Sales Pitch

> **Example:** If you have a quirky sense of humor, let that come through in your pitch. Your unique personality can make your pitch more memorable and relatable.

Share Personal Stories:
Personal stories and experiences can create a deeper connection with your audience. Share why you wrote the book, what inspired you, and any challenges you faced along the way.

> **Example:** "I was inspired to write 'The Forgotten Kingdom' after visiting an ancient archaeological site. The sense of history and mystery was overwhelming, and I knew I had to share that feeling with others through my writing."

Embrace Vulnerability:
Don't be afraid to show vulnerability in your pitch. Sharing your challenges, doubts, and growth can make you more relatable and human to your audience.

> **Example:** "Writing this book wasn't easy. There were times when I doubted myself and the story I was telling. But I persevered, and I'm proud of what I've created. I hope you find it as inspiring as I did."

Connect on a Human Level:
Remember that you're speaking to real people with their own emotions and experiences. Connect with your audience on a human level by acknowledging their feelings and experiences.

> **Example:** "I know we all love a good adventure and a story that takes us to another world. That's what I aimed to create with 'The Forgotten Kingdom.' A story that transports you and leaves you feeling like you've been on an incredible journey."

Be Consistent:
Ensure that your authenticity is consistent across all your interactions and platforms. Whether you're speaking at an event, posting on social media, or writing a blog post, maintain a consistent and genuine tone.

> **Example:** If you're known for being candid and approachable on social media, carry that same tone into your sales pitch and other promotional materials.

Show Appreciation:
Express genuine gratitude and appreciation for your audience's support. Acknowledging their role in your success can build a stronger connection and foster loyalty.

> **Example:** "Thank you for considering 'The Forgotten Kingdom.' Your support means the world to me, and I'm grateful for every reader who embarks on this journey with me."

Engage in Meaningful Conversations:
Engage with your audience in meaningful conversations. Listen to their feedback, respond to their comments, and show genuine interest in their thoughts and experiences.

> **Example:** Host a Q&A session on social media where you answer questions about your book and your writing process. Engage with readers and thank them for their questions and feedback.

Stay True to Your Values:
Stay true to your values and beliefs in your pitch. Authenticity comes from aligning your message with your core values and principles. Don't compromise your integrity for the sake of a sale.

Art of the Sales Pitch

>**Example:** If your book addresses important social issues, be clear about your stance and the values that guided your writing. Authenticity can resonate strongly with readers who share your values.

Chapter Summary: In this chapter, we explored the importance of being authentic in your sales pitch. By being honest and transparent, sharing your passion, using your unique voice, sharing personal stories, embracing vulnerability, connecting on a human level, being consistent, showing appreciation, engaging in meaningful conversations, and staying true to your values, you can create a sincere and trustworthy pitch. Authenticity helps build a genuine connection with your audience, making your message more relatable and persuasive, and increasing the likelihood of engaging potential readers and driving sales for your book.

11
What is an Elevator Pitch?

An elevator pitch is a concise, persuasive speech that you can use to spark interest in your book within a brief timeframe, typically 30 seconds to 2 minutes. Understanding and using it can lead to success. Here's how to craft and deliver an effective elevator pitch:

Keep It Short and Sweet:
An elevator pitch should be brief and to the point. Aim to convey the most important information about your book within 30 to 60 seconds. This means focusing on the essentials and avoiding unnecessary details.

> **Example:** "Hi, I'm [Your Name], author of 'The Forgotten Kingdom.' It's a thrilling historical fiction novel set in ancient Mesopotamia, where an archaeologist unravels a series of mysteries that could change our understanding of history."

Start with a Hook:
Begin with a hook that grabs attention and piques curiosity. Your hook should be intriguing and set the stage for what's to come.

> **Example:** "Imagine uncovering secrets buried for thousands of years, secrets that could rewrite history."

Clearly State the Value Proposition:
Clearly articulate the unique value of your book. What sets it apart from others in its genre? What will readers gain from it?

Art of the Sales Pitch

> **Example:** "'The Forgotten Kingdom' offers a unique blend of historical accuracy and gripping storytelling, perfect for fans of adventure and mystery."

Highlight Key Features:
Briefly highlight the key features of your book. This could include the genre, main plot points, unique aspects, or any special elements.

> **Example:** "The book features richly detailed historical settings, complex characters, and a plot full of twists and turns."

Include a Call-to-Action:
End your pitch with a clear call-to-action. Tell your audience what you want them to do next, whether it's buying your book, visiting your website, or following you on social media.

> **Example:** "If you love history and adventure, check out 'The Forgotten Kingdom.' You can find it on Amazon or at your favorite bookstore."

Practice Your Pitch:
Practice delivering your pitch until it feels natural and confident. Rehearse in front of a mirror, record yourself, or practice with friends. The more you practice, the more comfortable you'll become.

> **Example:** Record your pitch and play it back to identify areas for improvement. Adjust your tone, pace, and emphasis as needed.

Be Prepared to Adapt:
Be ready to adapt your pitch for different audiences and situations. Tailor your message to suit the interests and preferences of your audience.

Example: If you're pitching to a history enthusiast, emphasize the historical accuracy and research behind your book. If you're speaking to a general reader, focus on the adventure and excitement.

Use Confident Body Language:
When delivering your pitch in person, use confident body language. Maintain eye contact, stand tall, and use natural gestures to enhance your message.

Example: Practice delivering your pitch with a friend and ask for feedback on your body language. Make adjustments to ensure you appear confident and engaged.

Stay Positive and Enthusiastic:
Show enthusiasm for your book and its message. Positive energy can be contagious and can help engage your audience.

Example: Smile and use an enthusiastic tone when talking about your book. Your passion can help inspire interest and excitement.

Be Ready for Questions:
Be prepared to answer questions that might arise from your pitch. Anticipate common questions and have concise, informative responses ready.

Example: If someone asks about the inspiration for your book, be ready to share a brief story or anecdote that highlights your motivation and passion.

Chapter Summary: In this bonus chapter, we explored the concept of an elevator pitch and how to craft and deliver an effective one. By keeping it short and sweet, starting with a hook, clearly stating the value proposition, highlighting key

Art of the Sales Pitch

features, including a call-to-action, practicing your pitch, being prepared to adapt, using confident body language, staying positive and enthusiastic, and being ready for questions, you can create a compelling elevator pitch that sparks interest and engages potential readers. An effective elevator pitch can open doors and create opportunities for promoting your book and connecting with your audience.

12
Understand the Market

Conducting market research to understand current trends, competition, and potential gaps your book can fill is crucial for positioning your book strategically. Here's how to effectively understand the market and use this knowledge to your advantage:

Research Market Trends:
Stay informed about the latest trends in your genre and the publishing industry as a whole. Understanding what's popular and what's gaining traction can help you position your book more effectively.

>   **Example:** If historical fiction with strong female protagonists is trending, highlight this aspect of your book in your pitch and marketing materials.

Analyze Competitors:
Study the books that are similar to yours and analyze their marketing strategies, strengths, and weaknesses. Understanding your competition can help you identify opportunities to differentiate your book.

>   **Example:** Look at bestselling historical fiction novels and analyze their covers, blurbs, reviews, and promotional tactics. Identify what works well and what you can do differently.

Identify Your Niche:
Find a niche within your genre that your book can fill. A well-defined niche can help you target a specific audience more effectively and stand out in a crowded market.

Art of the Sales Pitch

> **Example:** If your historical fiction novel focuses on an obscure period or event, position your book as a unique offering that provides fresh insights into that era.

Understand Your Audience's Preferences:
Conduct surveys, polls, or focus groups to gather information about your audience's preferences and reading habits. Use this data to tailor your book and marketing strategy to meet their needs.

> **Example:** Survey readers to find out what they love about historical fiction. Use their feedback to highlight similar aspects in your book.

Monitor Industry Reports:
Read industry reports and publications to stay informed about market dynamics, sales trends, and emerging opportunities. This knowledge can help you make informed decisions about your book's positioning and marketing.

> **Example:** Use reports from sources like Publishers Weekly, The New York Times, and industry newsletters to stay updated on market trends and bestselling genres.

Use Online Tools:
Leverage online tools and platforms to conduct market research. Tools like Google Trends, Amazon Bestsellers lists, and Goodreads can provide valuable insights into what readers are looking for.

> **Example:** Use Google Trends to see how interest in historical fiction has changed over time and identify related keywords that are gaining popularity.

Engage with Reader Communities:

Participate in online communities and forums where your target audience gathers. Engaging with readers can provide firsthand insights into their preferences and interests.

> **Example:** Join Goodreads groups focused on historical fiction and participate in discussions. Pay attention to what readers are talking about and what they're looking for in a book.

Identify Market Gaps:
Look for gaps in the market that your book can fill. Identifying underserved areas or unmet needs can help you position your book as a unique and valuable offering.

> **Example:** If you notice a lack of historical fiction set in ancient Mesopotamia, position your book as filling that gap and providing readers with a fresh and unique perspective.

Test Your Concepts:
Before finalizing your book and marketing strategy, test your concepts with your target audience. Gather feedback on your cover design, blurb, and key selling points to ensure they resonate with readers.

> **Example:** Share different cover designs on social media and ask your followers to vote on their favorite. Use the feedback to choose a cover that appeals to your audience.

Adjust Your Strategy:
Use the insights gained from your market research to adjust your strategy. Be flexible and willing to make changes based on what you learn about the market and your audience.

Art of the Sales Pitch

> **Example:** If your research shows that readers prefer e-books over print books in your genre, focus more on promoting the digital version of your book.

Chapter Summary: In this chapter, we explored the importance of understanding the market to position your book strategically. By researching market trends, analyzing competitors, identifying your niche, understanding your audience's preferences, monitoring industry reports, using online tools, engaging with reader communities, identifying market gaps, testing your concepts, and adjusting your strategy, you can gain valuable insights into the market and use this knowledge to your advantage. Understanding the market helps you make informed decisions about your book's positioning and marketing, increasing the likelihood of success.

13
Develop a Strong Opening

Your opening statement is crucial for capturing attention and setting the tone for your pitch. A strong opening can draw in your audience and make them eager to hear more. Here's how to develop a compelling opening for your sales pitch:

Start with a Hook:
Begin with a hook that grabs attention and piques curiosity. Your hook should be intriguing, relevant, and set the stage for what's to come.

> **Example:** "What if everything you knew about ancient history was about to be turned upside down?"

Use a Compelling Question:
Asking a thought-provoking question can engage your audience and make them think about your book. It also sets up an immediate connection and interest in what you have to say.

> **Example:** "Have you ever wondered what secrets are buried beneath the sands of time?"

Share a Surprising Fact:
A surprising or little-known fact related to your book can capture attention and intrigue your audience. This can also establish your credibility and knowledge on the subject.

> **Example:** "Did you know that the ancient city of Uruk was once the largest city in the world, with over 50,000 inhabitants?"

Art of the Sales Pitch

Use a Powerful Quote:
A powerful quote that relates to your book's theme or message can set the tone and draw in your audience. Choose a quote that resonates with the essence of your book.

> **Example:** "As the great historian Herodotus once said, 'History is written by the victors.' But what about the stories that were never told?"

Paint a Vivid Picture:
Use descriptive language to paint a vivid picture in the minds of your audience. This can make your opening more engaging and memorable.

> **Example:** "Imagine standing in the heart of an ancient city, the air thick with the scent of spices, the streets bustling with merchants and artisans. This is the world of 'The Forgotten Kingdom.'"

Share a Personal Anecdote:
A personal story or experience related to your book can create an emotional connection and make your pitch more relatable.

> **Example:** "I first discovered the ancient ruins of Uruk on a trip to Iraq. The sense of history and mystery was overwhelming, and I knew I had to write about it."

Use a Bold Statement:
A bold or provocative statement can grab attention and make your audience want to learn more. Make sure it's relevant and sets the stage for your pitch.

> **Example:** "This book will change the way you see history."

Introduce Your Main Character:
If your book has a compelling main character, introduce them in your opening. A well-crafted character introduction can draw your audience into the story.

> **Example:** "Meet Dr. Emily Carter, a fearless archaeologist who will stop at nothing to uncover the secrets of the ancient world."

Set Up a Mystery:
Introducing a mystery or unanswered question can create intrigue and make your audience eager to learn more about your book.

> **Example:** "Deep beneath the sands of Mesopotamia lies a secret that could change the course of history. Will you uncover it?"

Establish the Stakes:
Highlight the stakes or the central conflict of your book in your opening. This can create a sense of urgency and make your audience invested in the outcome.

> **Example:** "In 'The Forgotten Kingdom,' the discovery of an ancient artifact threatens to unravel everything we know about history. The race is on to uncover the truth before it's too late."

Chapter Summary: In this chapter, we discussed the importance of developing a strong opening for your sales pitch. By starting with a hook, using a compelling question, sharing a surprising fact, using a powerful quote, painting a vivid picture, sharing a personal anecdote, using a bold statement, introducing your main character, setting up a mystery, and establishing the stakes, you can create an engaging and memorable opening. A strong opening captures attention and sets the tone for the rest of your pitch, making your audience

Art of the Sales Pitch

eager to hear more and increasing the likelihood of driving interest and sales for your book.

14
Address Potential Objections

Anticipating and addressing potential objections your audience might have can enhance your credibility and make your pitch more persuasive. By proactively addressing concerns, you can alleviate doubts and build trust. Here's how to effectively address potential objections in your sales pitch:

Identify Common Objections:
Consider the common objections or concerns your audience might have about your book. These could include doubts about the content, genre, pricing, or relevance. Make a list of potential objections to address.

Example: Common objections for a historical fiction novel might include concerns about historical accuracy, relevance, or the length of the book.

Address Objections Proactively:
Incorporate responses to potential objections directly into your pitch. Addressing concerns before they are raised shows that you understand your audience's perspective and are prepared to alleviate their doubts.

>**Example:** "I've spent years researching the ancient civilization of Mesopotamia to ensure the historical accuracy of 'The Forgotten Kingdom.' Every detail is meticulously crafted to bring the past to life."

Provide Evidence and Examples:
Use evidence and examples to support your responses to objections. This can include research findings, expert

Art of the Sales Pitch

endorsements, or specific examples from your book that address the concerns.

> **Example:** "This book has been endorsed by leading historians for its authenticity. Dr. Jane Doe, a renowned archaeologist, praised it for its accurate portrayal of ancient Mesopotamia."

Highlight Positive Reviews:
Use positive reviews and testimonials to counter objections. Feedback from other readers who have enjoyed your book can help build trust and credibility.

> **Example:** "Readers have described 'The Forgotten Kingdom' as a page-turner that combines rich historical detail with an engaging plot. One reviewer said, 'I couldn't put it down. It's like stepping back in time.'"

Offer Comparisons:
Compare your book to similar successful books in the genre to show its value. Highlight what makes your book unique while demonstrating that it meets the expectations of the genre.

> **Example:** "If you enjoyed 'The Nightingale' by Kristin Hannah, you'll love 'The Forgotten Kingdom.' It offers the same immersive historical experience with a unique twist."

Address Pricing Concerns:
If price is a potential objection, explain the value readers will get from your book. Highlight any special features, additional content, or unique aspects that justify the price.

> **Example:** "For the price of a coffee, you'll get a captivating journey through ancient history, meticulously

researched and beautifully written. Plus, it includes exclusive behind-the-scenes insights from the author."

Emphasize Benefits:
Focus on the benefits readers will gain from your book. Address how it meets their needs, solves their problems, or enhances their experience.

Example: "Beyond just a thrilling story, 'The Forgotten Kingdom' offers readers a deep dive into ancient history, providing both entertainment and education."

Use Analogies and Metaphors:
Analogies and metaphors can make complex objections easier to understand and address. Use them to simplify your responses and make them more relatable.

Example: "Think of 'The Forgotten Kingdom' as a time machine. Just as a time machine would transport you to another era, this book takes you on an unforgettable journey through ancient Mesopotamia."

Show Empathy:
Acknowledge your audience's concerns and show empathy. Demonstrating that you understand their perspective can build rapport and trust.

Example: "I understand that readers want accurate historical details and engaging storytelling. That's why I've made sure to balance both in 'The Forgotten Kingdom.'"

Invite Further Questions:
Encourage your audience to ask further questions or express any additional concerns. Being open to dialogue shows that you are confident in your book and willing to address any issues.

Art of the Sales Pitch

> **Example:** "If you have any questions or concerns about 'The Forgotten Kingdom,' feel free to ask. I'm here to help and provide any information you need."

Chapter Summary: In this chapter, we discussed the importance of addressing potential objections in your sales pitch. By identifying common objections, addressing them proactively, providing evidence and examples, highlighting positive reviews, offering comparisons, addressing pricing concerns, emphasizing benefits, using analogies and metaphors, showing empathy, and inviting further questions, you can effectively alleviate doubts and build trust with your audience. Addressing objections enhances your credibility and makes your pitch more persuasive, increasing the likelihood of engaging potential readers and driving sales for your book.

15
Leverage Networking Opportunities

Networking is a powerful tool for promoting your book and building connections in the publishing industry. Leveraging networking opportunities can help you reach a wider audience, gain valuable insights, and create lasting relationships. Here's how to effectively leverage networking opportunities to promote your book:

Attend Industry Events:
Participate in industry events such as book fairs, writers' conferences, and literary festivals. These events provide opportunities to meet other authors, publishers, agents, and potential readers.

> **Example:** Attend the annual BookExpo or local literary festivals to connect with industry professionals and showcase your book to a broader audience.

Join Writers' Organizations:
Become a member of writers' organizations and associations. These groups often offer networking events, workshops, and resources that can help you promote your book and develop your career.

> **Example:** Join organizations like the Authors Guild or the Society of Children's Book Writers and Illustrators (SCBWI) to access networking opportunities and professional development resources.

Participate in Online Communities:
Engage with online communities and forums related to writing and your book's genre. These platforms provide opportunities

Art of the Sales Pitch

to connect with other writers, share your work, and gain feedback.

>**Example:** Join Facebook groups for writers, participate in Twitter chats like #WritingCommunity, or engage with Goodreads groups to build connections and promote your book.

Collaborate with Other Authors:
Collaborate with other authors on joint projects, such as anthologies, blog tours, or social media campaigns. Collaboration can help you reach new audiences and benefit from shared promotional efforts.

>**Example:** Partner with other historical fiction authors for a joint book tour or a themed blog series that highlights each author's work.

Attend Local Book Clubs:
Reach out to local book clubs and offer to attend their meetings to discuss your book. Book clubs provide a captive audience of engaged readers who can become advocates for your book.

>**Example:** Contact local libraries or community centers to find book clubs interested in discussing historical fiction and offer to join their discussions.

Utilize Social Media:
Use social media platforms to network with other authors, industry professionals, and readers. Engage in conversations, share valuable content, and promote your book through your social media channels.

>**Example:** Use Twitter to participate in writing hashtags, connect with fellow authors on Instagram, and join LinkedIn groups related to the publishing industry.

Volunteer at Literary Events:
Volunteer at literary events and conferences to gain behind-the-scenes access and build relationships with key players in the industry. Volunteering can also provide valuable insights and learning opportunities.

> **Example:** Volunteer at your local literary festival or writers' conference to meet industry professionals and gain exposure for your book.

Host or Attend Book Signings:
Host your own book signings or attend book signings of other authors. Book signings provide opportunities to meet readers, sign copies of your book, and promote your work.

> **Example:** Arrange a book signing event at a local bookstore or library. Attend signings by other authors to network and learn from their promotional strategies.

Offer to Speak at Events:
Offer to speak at events such as literary panels, writing workshops, or community gatherings. Speaking engagements can establish you as an authority in your field and provide opportunities to promote your book.

> **Example:** Offer to lead a workshop on writing historical fiction at a local writers' conference or speak about your research process at a historical society meeting.

Follow Up and Maintain Connections:
After networking events, follow up with the contacts you've made. Send personalized messages, connect on social media, and maintain regular communication to build lasting relationships.

Art of the Sales Pitch

> **Example:** After meeting someone at a conference, send a follow-up email thanking them for the conversation and suggesting ways to stay in touch or collaborate in the future.

Chapter Summary: In this chapter, we discussed the importance of leveraging networking opportunities to promote your book and build connections in the publishing industry. By attending industry events, joining writers' organizations, participating in online communities, collaborating with other authors, attending local book clubs, utilizing social media, volunteering at literary events, hosting or attending book signings, offering to speak at events, and following up and maintaining connections, you can expand your network and reach a wider audience. Networking helps you build valuable relationships and gain exposure for your book, increasing the likelihood of success.

16
Utilize Digital Platforms

Digital platforms offer a wide range of tools and opportunities for promoting your book and reaching a global audience. By effectively utilizing these platforms, you can increase your book's visibility and engage with readers. Here's how to leverage digital platforms to promote your book:

Create an Author Website:
An author website serves as a central hub for your online presence. It should include information about your book, your biography, a blog, and contact details. Use your website to showcase your work and connect with readers.

> **Example:** Create a website with sections for your books, a blog where you share writing tips and updates, and a contact form for readers to reach out to you.

Use Social Media:
Social media platforms like Facebook, Twitter, Instagram, and LinkedIn provide opportunities to engage with readers, share content, and promote your book. Use these platforms to build a community and connect with your audience.

> **Example:** Share behind-the-scenes content, book updates, and engage with readers on Instagram. Use Twitter to participate in writing hashtags and connect with other authors.

Start a Blog:
A blog allows you to share your thoughts, insights, and updates with your readers. Regular blog posts can help you

Art of the Sales Pitch

build an audience, establish your authority, and promote your book.

> **Example:** Write blog posts about the historical research behind your book, your writing process, and character development. Share these posts on social media to attract readers.

Utilize Email Marketing:
Build an email list and send regular newsletters to your subscribers. Email marketing allows you to directly communicate with your audience, share updates, and promote your book.

> **Example:** Offer a free chapter of your book as an incentive for readers to join your email list. Send monthly newsletters with exclusive content, book news, and special offers.

Leverage Online Retailers:
Utilize online retailers like Amazon, Barnes & Noble, and Kobo to reach a global audience. Optimize your book's listing with a compelling blurb, keywords, and categories to increase discoverability.

> **Example:** Use Amazon's Author Central to create a detailed author profile, manage your book listings, and track sales data. Optimize your book's metadata to improve search rankings.

Participate in Online Book Communities:
Engage with online book communities such as Goodreads and LibraryThing. These platforms allow you to connect with readers, join discussions, and promote your book through giveaways and reviews.

Example: Create an author profile on Goodreads, join groups related to your genre, and participate in discussions. Host a Goodreads giveaway to attract new readers.

Use Video Content:
Create video content to promote your book and engage with your audience. Videos can include book trailers, author interviews, and behind-the-scenes content. Share these videos on social media and your website.

Example: Produce a book trailer that highlights the main plot points and themes of your book. Share the trailer on YouTube, Facebook, and Instagram.

Engage in Podcasting:
Participate in podcasts as a guest or start your own podcast. Podcasts provide a platform to share your story, discuss your book, and reach new audiences.

Example: Reach out to podcast hosts who interview authors and offer to be a guest. Share insights about your writing process, research, and the themes of your book.

Run Digital Ads:
Use digital advertising to promote your book to a targeted audience. Platforms like Facebook Ads, Google Ads, and Amazon Advertising allow you to create targeted campaigns based on demographics, interests, and behaviors.

Example: Run a Facebook ad campaign targeting readers who are interested in historical fiction. Use eye-catching visuals and a compelling call-to-action to attract clicks.

Host Virtual Events:

Art of the Sales Pitch

Host virtual events such as book launches, readings, and Q&A sessions. Virtual events allow you to connect with readers from around the world and promote your book in an interactive format.

> **Example:** Host a virtual book launch on Zoom or Facebook Live. Read excerpts from your book, answer reader questions, and offer special promotions for attendees.

Chapter Summary: In this chapter, we discussed the importance of utilizing digital platforms to promote your book and reach a global audience. By creating an author website, using social media, starting a blog, utilizing email marketing, leveraging online retailers, participating in online book communities, using video content, engaging in podcasting, running digital ads, and hosting virtual events, you can increase your book's visibility and engage with readers. Digital platforms provide powerful tools and opportunities to connect with your audience and promote your book effectively.

17
Measure and Improve

Tracking the effectiveness of your sales pitches and marketing efforts is crucial for understanding what works and making necessary adjustments. By measuring your performance and continually improving, you can optimize your strategies and achieve better results. Here's how to measure and improve your sales pitches and marketing efforts:

Set Clear Goals:
Define clear and measurable goals for your sales pitches and marketing efforts. Your goals could include increasing book sales, growing your email list, or improving engagement on social media.

> **Example:** Set a goal to increase book sales by 20% over the next three months or to gain 500 new email subscribers within six months.

Use Analytics Tools:
Leverage analytics tools to track the performance of your sales pitches and marketing campaigns. Tools like Google Analytics, social media insights, and email marketing analytics provide valuable data.

> **Example:** Use Google Analytics to track website traffic, user behavior, and conversion rates. Monitor social media engagement using platform-specific insights.

Monitor Key Metrics:
Identify and monitor key metrics that align with your goals. Common metrics include website traffic, conversion rates, email open rates, click-through rates, and social media engagement.

Art of the Sales Pitch

> **Example:** Track the number of visitors to your book's landing page, the conversion rate of visitors who make a purchase, and the engagement rate of your social media posts.

Gather Feedback:
Collect feedback from your audience to understand their preferences and experiences. Use surveys, polls, and direct interactions to gather insights that can inform your strategies.

> **Example:** Send a survey to your email subscribers asking for their feedback on your newsletters, content preferences, and any suggestions for improvement.

Conduct A/B Testing:
Use A/B testing to compare different versions of your sales pitches, marketing materials, and campaigns. This allows you to identify what works best and make data-driven decisions.

> **Example:** Test two different email subject lines to see which one generates a higher open rate. Compare the performance of different ad creatives to determine which one drives more conversions.

Analyze Sales Data:
Review your sales data to identify trends and patterns. Understanding which marketing efforts lead to increased sales can help you focus your resources on the most effective strategies.

> **Example:** Analyze your sales data to determine which channels generate the most sales. Identify peak sales periods and correlate them with specific marketing campaigns.

Adjust Your Strategy:

Based on your analysis and feedback, make adjustments to your sales pitches and marketing strategies. Be flexible and willing to experiment with new approaches to improve your results.

> **Example:** If you notice that email marketing generates the highest conversion rates, allocate more resources to growing your email list and optimizing your email campaigns.

Continuously Improve:
Strive for continuous improvement by regularly reviewing your performance and seeking opportunities to enhance your strategies. Stay informed about industry trends and best practices to stay ahead of the competition.

> **Example:** Attend webinars, read industry blogs, and participate in online courses to stay updated on the latest marketing trends and techniques.

Document Your Learnings:
Keep a record of your learnings and insights from your marketing efforts. Documenting your successes and challenges can help you replicate effective strategies and avoid repeating mistakes.

> **Example:** Create a marketing journal where you document the results of your campaigns, key learnings, and any adjustments you made. Use this journal as a reference for future campaigns.

Celebrate Your Successes:
Acknowledge and celebrate your successes, no matter how small. Recognizing your achievements can boost your motivation and provide valuable encouragement as you continue to improve.

Art of the Sales Pitch

Example: Celebrate reaching a milestone in book sales or achieving a significant increase in email subscribers. Share your successes with your audience to build excitement and engagement.

Chapter Summary: In this chapter, we discussed the importance of measuring and improving your sales pitches and marketing efforts. By setting clear goals, using analytics tools, monitoring key metrics, gathering feedback, conducting A/B testing, analyzing sales data, adjusting your strategy, continuously improving, documenting your learnings, and celebrating your successes, you can optimize your strategies and achieve better results. Measuring and improving your efforts helps you make data-driven decisions and enhances the effectiveness of your sales pitches and marketing campaigns, increasing the likelihood of success.

About the Author

B Alan Bourgeois began his writing journey at age 12, crafting screenplays for *Adam-12* as an outlet to develop his style. While he never submitted these works, the experience fueled his passion for storytelling. After following the conventional advice of pursuing a stable career, Bourgeois rediscovered his love for writing in 1989 through a community college class, leading to his first published short story. Since then, he has written over 48 short stories, published more than 10 books, including the award-winning *Extinguishing the Light*, and made his mark in the publishing world.

Recognizing the challenges authors face, Bourgeois founded Creative House Press in the early 2000s, publishing 60 books by other authors in five years and gaining insights into the industry's marketing needs. In 2011, he launched the Texas Authors Association, which grew to include two nonprofits promoting Texas writers and literacy. He also created innovative programs like the Lone Star Festival and short story contests for students, and in 2016, the Authors Marketing Event, offering a groundbreaking Certification program for book marketing expertise.

Despite setbacks during the COVID-19 pandemic, Bourgeois adapted by launching the Authors School of Business, providing essential tools for authors to succeed as "Authorpreneurs." As publishing evolves, he has explored NFTs as a potential revenue stream for writers. With decades of experience, Bourgeois remains a driving force in the literary community, committed to helping authors thrive in a changing industry.

Bourgeois is currently the director of the [Texas Authors Museum & Institute of History](), **based in Austin, Texas**

Art of the Sales Pitch

Other Books by the Author in this Series

Y'all Write: A Month-Long Guide to Achieving Your Writing Goals

Unlock your creative potential with *Y'all Write: A Month of Writing Celebration and Growth*! This guide offers tips, motivation, and tools to help writers of all levels set goals, build momentum, and embrace the joy of storytelling.

Author's Roadmap to Success: Proven Strategies for Thriving in Publishing

Unlock the secrets to literary success with *Author's Roadmap to Success: Proven Strategies for Thriving in Publishing*. This essential guide provides actionable strategies to help writers build strong habits, master self-publishing, and thrive in their writing careers.

The Writer's Self-Care Guide: Top Ten Steps to Balance and Thrive

Transform your writing journey with *The Writer's Self-Care Guide: Top Ten Steps to Balance and Thrive*. This practical guide offers actionable steps to nurture your creativity, set boundaries, and achieve a balanced, fulfilling writing life.

B Alan Bourgeois

Top Ten Keys for Successful Writing and Productivity

Unlock your writing potential with *Top Ten Keys for Successful Writing and Productivity*. This guide offers actionable strategies to build consistent habits, manage time effectively, and produce high-quality work to elevate your writing

Mastering Research: Top Ten Steps to Research Like a Pro

Elevate your writing with *Mastering Research: Top Ten Steps to Research Like a Pro*. This essential guide provides practical tools and techniques to conduct thorough, credible research and seamlessly integrate it into your work.

Character Chronicles: Crafting Depth and Consistency in Creative Projects

Bring your characters to life with *Character Chronicles: Crafting Depth and Consistency in Creative Projects*. This essential guide reveals professional techniques to develop authentic, complex characters that resonate across any creative medium.

Editing Essentials: Your Guide to Finding the Perfect Editor

Transform your manuscript with *Editing Essentials: Your Guide to Finding the Perfect Editor*. This guide provides practical steps to identify, evaluate, and collaborate with the ideal editor to elevate your writing.

Art of the Sales Pitch

AI Programs Apps Authors Should Use

Revolutionize your writing with *Top Ten AI Programs Authors Should Use*. This guide explores powerful AI tools like Grammarly and Scrivener, offering practical tips to enhance creativity, productivity, and efficiency.

The Business of Writing

Master the publishing world with *Unlocking the Business of Writing*. This essential guide provides expert advice and practical tips to build your author platform, maximize royalties, and turn your passion into a thriving career.

Creating an Effective Book Cover

Create a book cover that captivates readers with *Top Ten Keys to Creating an Effective Book Cover*. This guide offers expert tips and practical advice on design, branding, and marketing to make your book stand out.

Mastering the Art of the Sales Pitch

Master the art of the sales pitch with *Mastering the Art of the Sales Pitch*. This guide provides essential strategies to captivate your audience, highlight your book's value, and drive its success.

B Alan Bourgeois

Publishing Issues Authors Deal With

Overcome publishing challenges with *Top Ten Publishing Hurdles and How to Overcome Them*. This guide offers practical strategies and expert insights to help you navigate rejection, editing, marketing, and more to achieve your publishing dreams.

The Indie Author Advantage: Mastering Control, Royalties, and Reach for Self-Publishing Success

Thrive as an indie author with *The Indie Author Advantage: Mastering Control, Royalties, and Reach for Self-Publishing Success*. This guide offers actionable strategies to retain creative control, maximize royalties, and reach a global audience.

Mastering Amazon Publishing: A Comprehensive Guide to Success for Indie Authors

Achieve self-publishing success with *Mastering Amazon Publishing: A Comprehensive Guide to Success for Indie Authors*. This guide provides proven strategies to navigate KDP, boost visibility, and maximize earnings for your books.

Art of the Sales Pitch

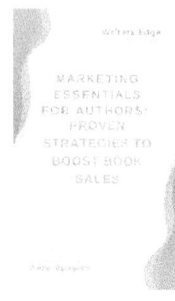

Marketing Essentials for Authors: Proven Strategies to Boost Book Sales

Boost your book sales with *Top Ten Marketing Essentials for Authors: Proven Strategies to Promote Your Book*. This guide combines traditional and digital marketing tactics to help authors effectively connect with readers and turn their books into bestsellers.

Marketing Mastery: Avoiding Common Mistakes for Authors

Master book marketing with *Marketing Mastery: Avoiding Common Mistakes for Authors*. This guide offers actionable advice to help authors connect with readers, build a strong online presence, and achieve their publishing goals.

The Author Branding Blueprint

Elevate your writing career with *Author Brand Mastery: A Comprehensive Guide to Building and Sustaining Your Unique Identity*. This guide provides practical steps to define your brand, build a professional presence, and connect meaningfully with your audience.

B Alan Bourgeois

Reader Magnet: Top Strategies for Building an Engaged Reader Community

Build a loyal reader community with *Reader Magnet: Top Strategies for Building an Engaged Reader Community*. This guide offers actionable strategies to connect with readers, create exclusive content, and turn your audience into passionate advocates.

Author Platform Mastery: A Comprehensive Guide to Building, Monetizing, and Growing Your Audience

Build your literary empire with *Author Platform Mastery: A Comprehensive Guide to Building, Monetizing, and Growing Your Audience*. This essential guide offers practical strategies to define your brand, engage readers, and expand your reach.

Networking Success for Authors: Essential Strategies Guide

Achieve your literary goals with *Networking Success for Authors: Essential Strategies Guide*. This practical roadmap offers strategies to build meaningful connections, promote your work, and create a supportive community for lasting success.

Art of the Sales Pitch

Write, Publish, Market: The Ultimate Handbook for Author Success
ISBN:
Master the modern publishing landscape with *Write, Publish, Market: The Ultimate Handbook for Author Success*. This guide provides actionable strategies to build your author brand, attract readers, and achieve long-term success in your writing career.

Mastering Interviews: Essential Tips for Authors' Success

Excel in interviews with *Mastering Interviews: Essential Tips for Authors' Success*. This guide offers practical advice to confidently promote your work, connect with audiences, and turn every interview into a memorable success.

Mastering Event Presentations: Avoiding Common Author Mistakes

Captivate your audience with *Mastering Event Presentations: Avoiding Common Author Mistakes*. This guide offers practical strategies to avoid pitfalls, engage your audience, and deliver impactful presentations that boost your confidence and connect with readers.

B Alan Bourgeois

Survival Strategies for Indie Authors: Overcoming Challenges and Achieving Success

Thrive as an indie author with *Survival Strategies for Indie Authors: Overcoming Challenges and Achieving Success*. This guide provides practical advice and actionable tips to overcome obstacles, enhance your skills, and achieve your publishing goals.

Empowering Authors: Top Ten Strategies for Writing Success and Career Growth

Achieve your writing dreams with *Empowering Authors: Top Ten Strategies for Writing Success and Career Growth*. This guide offers practical advice and proven strategies to build habits, refine your craft, and grow your author career with confidence.

The Sacred Connection

Infuse your writing with mindfulness and purpose through *Creating with Spirit: The Sacred Art of Writing and Publishing*. This guide transforms your creative journey into a spiritual practice, empowering you to inspire readers and overcome challenges with authenticity and intention.

Art of the Sales Pitch

Beyond the Basics: Advanced Strategies for Indie Author Success
ISBN:
Elevate your indie publishing career with *Beyond the Basics: Advanced Strategies for Indie Author Success*. This guide offers actionable tips and strategies to diversify income, engage readers, and build a sustainable, thriving career.

The AI Author: Embracing the Future of Fiction

Embrace the future of storytelling with *The AI Author: Balancing Efficiency and Creativity in Fiction Writing*. This guide helps authors harness AI to boost productivity and creativity while preserving the emotional depth and artistry of creating.

The Non-Fiction Nexus: Balancing AI and Human Insight in the Future of Writing

Elevate your non-fiction writing with *The Non-Fiction Nexus: Balancing AI and Human Insight in the Future of Writing*. This guide shows how to harness AI's efficiency while preserving the creativity and ethical judgment that make your work truly impactful.

B Alan Bourgeois

Authorship Reimagined: NFTs and Blockchain Essentials
ISBN:
Embrace the future of publishing with *NFT and Blockchain Essentials for Authors' Success*. This guide explains how blockchain and NFTs can protect your work, automate royalties, and expand your audience while maximizing revenue.

Adapting Success: Your Book's Journey to Film

Turn your book into a cinematic sensation with *From Page to Screen: A Step-by-Step Guide to Adapting Your Book into a Blockbuster Film*. This guide provides practical advice and industry insights to help you navigate the adaptation process and bring your story to life on the big screen.

Beyond the Basics: Advanced Strategies for Indie Author Success
Elevate your indie publishing career with this ultimate guide to mastering advanced strategies in writing, marketing, and global distribution. Packed with actionable tips and real-world examples, it empowers authors to balance creativity with entrepreneurship and build sustainable, thriving careers.

Art of the Sales Pitch

2026: The Ultimate Year for Indie Authors

Make 2026 your breakthrough year with *The Ultimate Year for Indie Authors*. This guide offers practical strategies to optimize publishing, leverage social media, and achieve unparalleled success in your indie author journey.